GOOD
KARMA

WHAT YOU GIVE YOU GET BACK

Published by Hinkler Books Pty Ltd
45–55 Fairchild Street
Heatherton Victoria 3202 Australia
www.hinkler.com

hinkler

Author: Nevill Drury
Internal design: Lisa Robertson
Cover design: Maria Daley

Images © Shutterstock.com

ISBN: 978 1 4889 2203 9

Printed and bound in Malaysia

GOOD
KARMA

WHAT YOU GIVE YOU GET BACK

Nevill Drury

hinkler

CONTENTS

Karma is the eternal
assertion of human
freedom… Our
thoughts, our words and
deeds are the threads
of the net which we
throw around ourselves.

Swami Vivekanda

Introducing Good Karma

We have all heard the expression 'good karma', but what does it really mean? Expressed very simply, the Eastern concept of karma is based on the principle of cause and effect – the idea that for every action there is an equal and opposite reaction. All of us recognise this principle in the physical, everyday world, and most of us also acknowledge that our own personal actions and decisions will have specific consequences – that what we do now will have a spin-off effect further down the line.

However, the universal law of karma extends beyond the physical world into the mental, emotional and spiritual aspects of life as well. The concept of karma applies not only to physical actions, but to every conscious thought and action that arises in our everyday lives. According to the karmic philosophy of life, positive thoughts and actions produce a positive outcome and create good karma. Negative thoughts and actions result in negative outcomes and create bad karma. We literally create our own individual futures by weaving karmic outcomes from the threads of our individual thoughts and actions.

A common misconception in the West is that the so-called 'law of karma' equates with the idea of fate, that somehow – by the time we are born – the universe has already mapped out our life events and circumstances ahead of time. As we will see, this is not the case. The law of karma proposes that we are very much masters of our own destiny, that we ourselves help to shape this destiny. Whether or not we accumulate good karma along the way is entirely up to us.

From this perspective, we should consider our life on this Earth as a spiritual adventure. The law of karma provides us with a context for our personal journey and also, along the way, teaches us how to act ethically and morally and with respect for all sentient creatures. When we learn the lessons of karma, we learn the lessons of life itself. Creating good karma is something we can do not only for ourselves, but for the well-being of humanity as a whole.

What is Karma?

The Eastern concept of karma is based on the principle of cause and effect. In Western society, we recognise this principle as an axiom of modern physics. If we apply heat or pressure to a physical object, we achieve an immediate effect, and this effect is directly related to the nature of our action. For example, if we heat ice it will melt, and if we prick a balloon with a pin it will burst and so on. Similarly, if we roll a ball along the ground it will keep rolling as long as we apply force or pressure to keep it in motion. All of us recognise such examples of cause and effect in the physical, everyday world. However, in the East, the idea of cause and effect is applied on a more far-reaching basis, and extends beyond the physical world into the mental, emotional and spiritual domains as well. The universal law of karma applies not only to physical cause and effect, but to every conscious thought and action that arises in our lives.

Good and bad karma

The basic principle that underpins the spiritual law of karma is both simple and direct. According to the karmic philosophy of life, positive thoughts and actions produce a positive outcome and create good karma. Negative thoughts and actions result in negative outcomes and create bad karma. This means we can never escape from ourselves, or at least from the consequences of our thoughts, emotions and actions. Every minute of every day, we are creating an ongoing stream of good and bad karma. You may already be thinking that this seems like a rather daunting idea, and indeed, in one sense, it is. The compensation, however, is that, according to the Eastern wisdom traditions in which the concept of karma has its origin, the law of karma applies equally and consistently to everyone – without exception. In the West, we often say 'what goes around, comes around' or we may recall the biblical teaching that each of us must reap what we sow. This is really the same idea as karma, expressed slightly differently. Karma isn't so much a judgment on who and what we are, but rather a way of seeing how each of us has an impact on one another, as well as on our own present life-situation, through our thoughts, deeds and emotions.

Is karma like fate?

The Sanskrit word karma is usually translated as 'action', but it has also been translated as 'work'. The overriding idea is that each of us must work out our karma through the actions we undertake in our lives. Some people think this means that karma is like fate, and that we have to live our lives according to what our fate has in store for us. However, this is not the true meaning of karma because it is widely recognised in the Eastern spiritual traditions that each of us can and should take responsibility for what we think and do, even if we are experiencing personal hardships or difficulties. The law of karma does not imply that our future is laid out for us, or that our lives are somehow predestined. Rather, it emphasises that we are the way we are, and find ourselves in our present situation, as a direct result of what we have thought or done at an earlier time. Because Eastern spiritual traditions like Hinduism and Buddhism maintain that each of us has lived many lives on this earth before – and that any individual life is really nothing other than a journey of the soul – the idea of karma is traditionally linked to the cyclic concept of birth, death and rebirth. The 'earlier time' we have mentioned in terms of karmic cause and effect could then be related not only to thoughts and events in our present lifetime, but also to what took place during a previous incarnation. According to this teaching, the conscious thoughts and deeds of our former lives affect the nature of our present life on earth, and our present thoughts and actions will in turn affect the nature of our future lives to come. In the Eastern spiritual perspective, we can never be truly free until we liberate ourselves from the ongoing cycle of karma.

What if I don't believe in reincarnation?

Many people in the West dislike the idea that their present lives may have been influenced by previous existences; many also reject the idea of reincarnation, or spiritual rebirth, out of hand. Some react critically to the very idea that we live in the country of our birth, have the parents we have, and find ourselves in a situation of wealth or poverty, health or ill-health, as a result of previous incarnations. For some, the whole idea of karma seems negative and even fatalistic. However, as we have already seen, karma does not imply that we are trapped in our present situation. Even if we don't believe in reincarnation, we can nevertheless adopt an ethical standard of personal conduct as advocated by the law of karma. Similarly, we can use positive thoughts, acts and intentions to change the quality of our lives and the nature of our interactions with other people. We can indeed become masters of our own destiny if we begin to take responsibility for how we treat those around us while acknowledging the consequences of how we think and behave in our everyday lives. As we will see, the idea of creating good karma depends on taking complete personal responsibility for our present situation. It involves recognising our strengths as well as acknowledging our weaknesses and vulnerabilities, then making a positive decision to act ethically, morally and spiritually in our everyday lives. If we are really serious about it, the time for creating good karma starts right now.

Karma in Eastern Religions

If we are to understand the true concept of karma we need to know how Eastern concepts of spirituality differ from those in the West.

One of the major distinctions between the major Eastern and Western religions is that Eastern religions like Hinduism and Buddhism emphasise endless cycles of cosmic time without beginning or end, in which the Universe and all living beings experience countless transformations. Western religions like Judaism, Christianity and Islam, on the other hand, conceive of the Creation, followed by a spiritual revelation, and then a Final Judgment. Put simply, Eastern religions embrace infinite cycles of time, whereas Western religions deal with finite beginnings and endings. This produces a very different style of religious belief. In the East, it is taken for granted that an individual has many lifetimes to achieve spiritual liberation, whereas in the West, only one opportunity – this lifetime – exists to achieve personal salvation for all eternity.

Karma and reincarnation

As mentioned earlier, the concept of karma is closely associated with the idea of reincarnation. The belief that each of us may already have lived many lives on this earth, with many more yet to unfold, is widely accepted in the East – by Hindus, Buddhists, Sikhs and Jains alike. Many Hindus believe also in the possibility of regression – that human beings can reincarnate as animals if their karma dictates it – but Buddhists generally believe that once a soul has achieved human status, the path of spiritual development continues ever-upward towards spiritual release, and it is unlikely that a human being will revert to an animal form.

During the night when he became enlightened, Gautama Buddha is said to have experienced many of his own previous lives, so was able to accept the truth of spiritual rebirth. Belief in spiritual rebirth is also accepted by the Dalai Lama. In his memoirs, *My Land and My People*, the Dalai Lama mentions that it was his belief in karma and reincarnation that sustained him during the Chinese invasion of Tibet, helping him to embrace compassion in the face of tragedy. 'Belief in rebirth should engender a universal love,' he writes in his memoir, '… and the virtues our creed encourages are those which arise from this universal love – tolerance, forbearance, charity, kindness, compassion … If there is no peace in one's mind, there can be no peace in one's approach to others, and thus no peaceful relations between individuals or between nations.'

Even though belief in reincarnation and karma is widespread in the East, different points of emphasis in the different spiritual traditions nevertheless exist. Following is a brief summary of some of the similarities and differences.

Karma in Different Spiritual Traditions

Hinduism

Hindu devotees generally believe that everything in our present lifetime has been shaped and brought about by the actions committed in a previous lifetime. The law of karma affects not only the individual person through all of his or her many lives, but also has an impact on the Hindu gods and goddesses as well. The endless flow of life, death and rebirth is referred to in the Hindu tradition as samsara, which means 'stream' or 'current'. The Katha Upanishad says: 'Man is caught in the stream... and like wheat man ripens [and dies] and like grain he is born again.' From the Hindu point of view, each specific lifetime and individual personality is regarded rather like a new set of clothes occupied by the eternal soul. As the soul progresses through each lifetime, it casts off one set of clothes and acquires a new set. This process is governed by the law of karma.

Buddhism

There are two main schools of Buddhism, known as Mahayana and Hinayana (or Theraveda). Mahayana Buddhism is found in northern India, Nepal, Japan and Tibet, whereas Hinayana Buddhism is more common in southeast Asia, and is found in such countries as Thailand, Sri Lanka, Laos and Burma. Hinayana Buddhists follow sacred Buddhist texts written in Pali rather than in Sanskrit, and spell the word karma as 'kamma'. The two branches of Buddhism have a slightly different perspective on spiritual rebirth and spiritual liberation, with Hinayana Buddhists tending to downplay the significance of mystical and visionary experiences, preferring instead to focus more on the practical and ethical aspects of Gautama Buddha's teachings.

For MAHAYANA BUDDHISTS, karma is a universal law from which there is no escape. Each human being inherits the karma of past lives and creates further karma during the present lifetime – all of which affects future rebirths. Mahayana Buddhists believe it is possible to break free from the patterns caused by karma, but this can only come about by personal good works, thoughts and actions – prayer, sacrifice and ritual offerings are not enough. Among Mahayana Buddhists, the only exception to this pattern of belief is found in the so-called 'Pure Lands' school of Buddhism in Japan and China, in which faith in the Amida Buddha is more important than engaging in good works in the pursuit of spiritual salvation.

HINAYANA BUDDHISTS emphasise that the world is in a continual process of flux and change, with no creation and no destruction, no beginning and no end. Even one's own individual identity is really an illusion. The chain of kamma can only be broken by rising above the universal cycle of cause and effect, then making it cease altogether.

Sikhs

Sikhs follow Hindu beliefs about karma, but believe that spiritual release from the cycles of rebirth comes both from one's own individual efforts and also from the grace of God. According to Guru Nanak, who founded the Sikh movement in the 16th century, the individual who seeks spiritual enlightenment through personal effort will be continually reborn; only through God's grace can a human being achieve final spiritual liberation.

Jains

Followers of the ancient Indian Jain sect maintain that their tradition is even older than Hinduism. Their main spiritual figurehead is Mahavira, who was a contemporary of Gautama Buddha. However, Mahavira was not their founder. Jains do not regard karma as an abstract moral principle in the universe, but as something material that ties the soul to the world and its attractions. Jains believe that karma cannot be detected through the senses. However, they maintain that individual karma can be 'burned up' if one follows certain austerities like fasting.

Bringing Karma into Everyday Living

Although different perspectives on karma can be found in the various branches of Eastern religion, the important thing to remember is that the concept of karma is always applied as a philosophy of practical action. According to the Eastern wisdom traditions, karma is not only a spiritual law, but also a principle that by its very nature demands well-intentioned and ethical conduct. Recognising the cause-and-effect impact of karma on both ourselves and others is something that we can bring into our everyday lives.

In subsequent chapters of this book, we will explore how the karmic philosophy teaches us to watch not only our actions, but also our thoughts and emotions. However, before we move on to discuss these particular topics, it is worth considering some of the key ideas propounded by Gautama Buddha, since his philosophy of life has had a direct bearing on how we have come to view karma in the West.

Dealing with suffering and unhappiness

Gautama Buddha always maintained that he was simply a human being, at no time claiming to be a god. However, he is now widely acknowledged as one of the most enlightened human beings who ever lived – and he became enlightened during the course of his own lifetime. For Buddha, this state of awakened awareness involved penetrating through to the true nature of the human condition and to the root causes of human suffering and unhappiness.

Buddha's main teaching focused on the so-called 'four noble truths', which can be summarised as follows:

- Life involves suffering
- The cause of this suffering is desire
- Suffering can be eliminated when desire is removed
- There is a path that leads to the elimination of suffering and this is known as the eightfold path. It comprises:
  - Right understanding
  - Right speech
  - Right vocation
  - Right mindfulness
  - Right aspiration
  - Right conduct
  - Right effort
  - Right concentration

Buddha believed that every human being should become aware of the connection between cause and effect, or the law of karma, because if we experience something negative in our lives – something that is causing unhappiness or some other form of suffering – the way to deal with it is by eradicating the cause of that suffering. According to Buddha, we can only attain a true state of inner and outer harmony by considerable personal effort aimed at spiritual self-transformation. This, in turn, involves striving to see the world clearly, responding to those around us without judgment, without envy, and without hatred. Buddha maintained that in order to achieve these things, we would have to learn to know ourselves intimately, and to experience the ultimate source of the happiness or unhappiness within us. Buddha himself did not believe in spiritual or religious dogma, advising his followers not to take his word simply on trust. It was more a matter of putting the karmic principles to the test. 'You yourself must make the effort,' he told his devotees, 'for Buddhas only point the way.'

As a way of recognising the law of karma in everyday life, Buddha advocated what have come to be known as the 'five precepts'; these can be stated succinctly:

1. I undertake to refrain from harming living things.
2. I undertake to refrain from taking what is not given.
3. I undertake to refrain from a misuse of the senses.
4. I undertake to refrain from wrong speech.

The first of these precepts means that we should show respect to all living creatures – the principle of tolerance and compassion should be extended not only to human beings, but to all living things. The second precept is the Buddhist equivalent of the familiar biblical teaching: 'Thou shalt not steal', but with the added inference that we should wait until things are offered rather than seize them out of self-interest because we desire them or have become attached to them. The third precept is really about learning to respect our bodies and our faculties of awareness, because it is through our physical senses that we come to know and experience the world in which we live. Buddha is not saying that we should not enjoy the various dimensions of physical awareness that our senses present to us; rather, he is reminding us that our senses are not there to be abused.

The sorts of 'wrong speech' Buddha had in mind with his fourth precept included lying, slander, backbiting, gossip, and malicious talk intended to stir up hatred or violence – the sort of 'wrong speech' that continues to stir up anger and hostility in everyday modern life! In his final precept, Buddha asked his followers not to cloud their minds with either drugs or drink, because one of his key teachings was that we all need to see things as they really are: in order to truly understand the nature of the human condition, we need to remove the veils of illusion that surround and imprison us.

Gautama Buddha's teachings can be condensed still further, often being presented as three key axioms:

- Cease to do evil
- Learn to do good
- Purify your own mind

From the viewpoint of the law of karma, these three axioms should be applied not only to the way we act in the world, but also to our thoughts and emotions, because the latter arise as a result of our personal intentions.

Put simply, if we wish to build good karma, we should cease to do evil, learn to do good, and strive to purify our minds. This, of course, is easier said than done – but we can make a start. As we said earlier, for each and every one of us creating good karma begins right now.

Watching Our Actions

One very specific way of relating to the idea of karma is by becoming increasingly aware of the consequences of our own actions. As someone once observed, karma can be regarded as 'action plus the results of action'. So, if you are mean or spiteful to someone you are dealing with, or if you deliberately cause hurt or injury to another person, or if you act in a way that disadvantages someone at work – perhaps by getting them to take the blame for something that you have done – all of this amounts to an accumulation of bad karma.

Alternatively, if, through your own personal actions, you do something to assist someone else, and you do it simply to help the person without expecting any reward or benefit in return, such an action is said to accumulate good karma. Perhaps you paused to help a frail and elderly person across the street, or ran errands for someone who was sick or incapacitated. Maybe you gave good and useful advice over the phone to someone whom you didn't even know but who could potentially benefit from your knowledge. These types of actions accumulate good karma because they are generous and essentially selfless. No doubt many such actions would reflect how most reasonable people would behave anyway – such actions would simply be the right thing to do. After all, most of us are willing to help someone if we are given the opportunity to do so, and most of us would act in this way without giving the matter a second thought.

Nevertheless, although we might consider many such incidences comparatively minor in themselves, in the karmic universe these actions still have an effect. They build into a stream of positive and negative consequences, a gradual accumulation that flows like a tide into our future lives and personal circumstances. According to the law of karma, what goes around comes around.

Karmic consequences

Sometimes the concept of karma sounds like an endless mathematical equation – a few pluses here, followed by a couple of minuses there. Although no mathematician is on hand actually keeping a tally, the law of karma does indeed seem to work like this on a basic level.

Sometimes we do something with bad intent and, according to the karmic law, if we then begin to repeat this pattern such actions will eventually take a personal toll on our state of well-being. The concept of 'karmic debt' is commonly referred to in the mystical literature, and what the wisdom teachings have in mind here is that the sum accumulation of our negative actions begins to pervade our individual consciousness.

Most of us are prone to certain habits, and some of these become 'bad habits' – an ingrained aspect of our personality. Perhaps we have gotten into the habit of telling little white lies; these then begin to multiply so that comparatively minor lies then become major falsehoods and deceptions. Maybe we have allowed ourselves to become easily irritated by minor problems, then allow this irritation to accumulate so that our irritation finally becomes a mounting anger accompanied by bursts of physical violence directed against another person. These are all examples of a rising karmic debt followed by the consequences of that negative accumulation.

According to the law of karma, all our actions result in an accumulated expression of their consequences, and the net effect of our actions can be either positive or negative – for the law of karma itself is neutral and impartial. An accumulation of negative actions builds into a negative personal cost, whereas an accumulation of positive actions will lead to a build-up of individual positive energy. In the latter case, according to the karmic philosophy, such benefits will in time flow through into the present or future life of the person who has built up such good karma.

Human differences

Someone once asked Gautama Buddha why different people showed different characteristics and qualities. Why was it that someone died in old age while another person died during youth? Why are some people rich and others poor? Why are some people more gifted or intelligent than others?

Buddha's response was that our present actions determine our future characteristics. Abstaining from killing leads to a longer life – if we take the life of other creatures (including insects!) our own lives will be shortened. If we act in a way than doesn't harm others, said Buddha, then we will be more healthy because hurtful actions create the karmic consequence of disease. Persistent anger and hatred provide the karmic conditions for ugliness, whereas acting with loving care and gentleness is likely to result in personal beauty. Actions pursued in a spirit of generosity lead karmically to wealth and abundance, whereas persistent greed will lead karmically to poverty.

Simply expressed, the law of karma affirms that if we act in a way that will bring happiness to others, we will find ourselves sooner or later in a fortunate physical environment with an increased opportunity for spreading happiness and good will. If, on the other hand, we cause pain to others through our individual actions or by failing to act when positive action was required, we will eventually find ourselves in unhappy surroundings. The reason for this is that karma provides us with the lessons we need for our own personal development. Karma ensures that we continue to reap the consequences of our actions until we learn through personal experience to acquire a greater wisdom in the way we live.

Dharma and opportunity

It has been said that action is the very essence of life. We engage in many different activities every day of our lives, but at the same time it is up to us to decide whether our lives and actions are meaningful and fruitful – and whether our actions are driven by selfish concerns or intended to benefit others. Our unfulfilled desires and our repressed wishes will be with us wherever we go in life, and for some people the failure to express such intentions through personal action becomes an ever-increasing burden.

One of the main purposes of the Eastern karmic philosophy of life is to lead people towards what we may regard as 'properly guided action' or 'right action'. In Buddhism, this is known as dharma, or living your life in accordance with the spiritual principles of the Universe. In the West, we might call it 'doing God's will'. In the East, it means conducting your life and assuming responsibility for your actions in a way that will lead to self-fulfilment and spiritual liberation.

According to karmic philosophy, our lives and actions provide us with numerous opportunities. Very often, the consequences of our karma will not be felt immediately. It has been said that karma is like a seed that lies dormant and seemingly inactive, but then finally sprouts, matures, and yields a harvest that can be reaped. This has been very well expressed in a small pamphlet recently released by the Theosophical Society, an organisation dedicated to bringing Eastern wisdom to the West: 'In the fertile soil of our physical, emotional and mental natures we plant the seeds of our future, and we carry with us the rich harvest of many past sowings. If the harvest seemingly is poor and unfruitful, it can be improved by planting better seed. We are never without opportunities to plant anew, to plant the seeds of love, of kindness, or beauty – that we may reap the harvest of tolerance, faith and loveliness.'

Watching Our Thoughts and Emotions

According to the law of karma, our thoughts and emotions are just as significant as our actions. After all, we tend to act on the basis of what we think is appropriate in a particular situation, and our state of conscious awareness will often lead us to formulate specific intentions. If our thoughts towards another person are well-intentioned, we will respond to them with openness, kindness and support. If, on the other hand, our thoughts are ill-intentioned, we may respond emotionally in a manner that is devious, deceptive or hostile. Clearly, how we think and how we act are interconnected, meaning that our thoughts, as well as our actions, can result in good or bad karma. As with our actions, the karmic impact of our thoughts is entirely up to us!

Gautama Buddha used to tell his monks: 'It is mental volition that I call karma. Having willed, one acts through body, speech or mind.' According to Buddhist tradition, all thoughts, actions and speech have their origins in either wholesome or unwholesome consciousness. If our thoughts are formulated on the basis of generosity, compassion or insight, our actions will then produce beneficial effects resulting in good karma. If, on the other hand, our thoughts are based on greed, hatred or delusion, this will result in undesirable or harmful effects and an accumulation of bad karma. The key to all of this is that we should try to cultivate positive states of conscious awareness that will eliminate delusion and suffering. Of course, this does not happen overnight; we cannot expect to transform our personalities without substantial personal effort and a considerable amount of deep self-exploration. Some specific suggestions for getting started on the path to personal transformation will be made in the next chapter; in the meantime, it may be worth taking a little time to reflect on how each of us can become captive to our negative thoughts and emotions – and how these, in turn, become barriers to our personal growth and to our sense of happiness and fulfilment.

Our thoughts and emotions provide a context for our actions in everyday life, especially in relation to our family, friends and work colleagues. Our thoughts and emotional responses towards other people also say a lot about how we view ourselves. Are we basically happy, fulfilled, at peace with ourselves, relaxed in the company of others, willing and able to provide emotional and compassionate support to those who are in need of such help? Or, by way of contrast, do we find ourselves forever lunging from one state of inner conflict to another, distracted by our focus on material possessions or the quest for power, wealth or recognition? Do our lives lack a sense of purpose, meaning or authenticity? Do we find ourselves unable to commit emotionally to another person on a deep level of intimacy? Are we forever on the defensive amidst the aggressive and competitive forces of modern society? Do we find ourselves caught up in states of unresolved anger and hostility that we then project onto those around us?

Certainly, most of us have experienced emotional states like this at one time or another, and from the karmic perspective, the reason is clear: we have brought these conditions upon ourselves! If we are miserable, or suffering on a mental or emotional level, it is because we have been seized by the power and consequences of our own negative thoughts.

Let us imagine ourselves in the corporate workplace for a moment. A person heavily conflicted with negative emotions, like greed and envy, might find herself drawn towards a prestigious and quite possibly unattainable corporate position with a high salary and a variety of glamorous privileges. She might also find herself becoming jealous of someone who had already attained such a position, while simultaneously despising herself for underachieving in the corporate workplace. On the other hand, a person less driven by greed and envy might find herself balancing the allure of wealth and power against the accompanying stresses and pressures that would inevitably come with the job. Quality of life considerations would come into play as a counterbalance to the forces of envy, jealousy or material greed. A healthy and balanced emotional perspective would enable the person to explore her present situation and accept things as they are without endlessly craving other possibilities, and making herself feel restless, unfulfilled or unhappy.

From a karmic point of view, people who are calm, happy and peaceful have managed to focus awareness on their true spiritual centres. They have found the centre of true inner knowing – that special place of harmony and well-being where they feel essentially at one with the forces of their own personal universe as well as with the world at large. Their lives have gained purpose and direction, with meaning and significance, reflecting a true and ongoing sense of relationship. By contrast, the unresolved and conflicted state of mind results in a lack of openness and connection – and an absence of spiritual focus. An accumulation of negative thoughts and actions results instead in a karmic mind-set dominated by doubts, anxiety, hostility and other alienating influences.

Acknowledging the dynamics of the law of karma provides us with the opportunity to understand the true nature of our desires and attachments. It enables us to reflect on the things we think will make us happy – and to help us place these considerations in their correct perspective. By seeking our inner spiritual centre while exploring the nature of our thoughts, aspirations and emotions, we gradually come to know who we are, as well as what we are seeking in our lives. As the Dalai Lama once said during one of his many lectures, 'our real battle takes place within ourselves'. We can only achieve spiritual liberation by harnessing and then eliminating the conflict of negative emotions. If we achieve this, we will then experience genuine and ongoing peace of mind.

Releasing Ourselves from Negativity

A good way to start creating good karma is to release yourself from negative thoughts, emotions and actions, although this will require persistence and an ongoing personal commitment. The process will also be greatly helped if you can learn to centre yourself spiritually, initially through relaxation, then by practising some form of meditation or visualisation that suits your own individual purpose. Adopting an open and positive frame of mind – perhaps assisted by personal affirmations – will help create the right physical and emotional context for your own personal development. You may like to begin this process by practising a relaxing 'white light' visualisation.

White Light Relaxation

Sit comfortably on the floor or in a chair, loosen any items of clothing that are likely to provide either distraction or discomfort, then begin progressively to relax different parts of your body. You might like to begin by visualising in your mind's eye that your feet are becoming increasingly limp and relaxed, then your ankles and your calves have also relaxed in turn. Imagine now that your legs are completely relaxed, and that a soothing feeling of relaxation has entered your abdomen and is working its way into your upper body. Now your chest is becoming completely relaxed and you are breathing deeply and without restriction. Finally, relax your arms, allowing the focus of your attention to remain solely in your head. Keep your focus on awareness itself, and imagine now that your head is filled with pure, radiant white light.

Now expand this field of pure white light and feel it moving gradually back down through all parts of your body. Visualise this stream of light passing down through your neck, into your chest, along your arms, and back down into your abdomen. Now imagine that it is extending down into your legs, finally reaching the soles of your feet. Finally, all of your body is filled with pure white light … Now, take a little time to experience the soothing qualities of this healing light, as it helps you to feel completely at ease with yourself. Stay with this deeply comforting and relaxing feeling, and then when you are ready, open your eyes and gradually return to your everyday awareness.

Centre yourself through your breath

Once you have practised this white light visualisation, you might also like to practise concentrating on the rhythm of your breathing. We all recognise instinctively that the way we breathe is important in helping us to relax our body and release any emotional blocks or anxieties that are inhibiting our flow of awareness. As part of developing our skills with breathing, we should also learn to focus on the nature of breathing itself, by listening closely to its repetitive patterns, engaging with the rhythm of our pulse and heartbeat, and becoming aware of the passage of air as we breathe slowly in and out through our nostrils. We can even visualise our breath, seeing it as a stream of energy flowing into every part of the body and then finally flowing free again.

For example, as a variation on the practice described above, you may find it useful to visualise your breath as a stream of pure white light, entering through the crown of your head, then forming a vortex as it passes down through your body. As you do this, imagine that each intake of breath is bringing new life and vitality to every cell in your body, and that each corresponding out-breath is removing anxieties or other negative emotions.

Don't allow your mind to wander or create any distractions. If you find that your powers of concentration are wavering, bring your focus back to the essential in-out rhythm of your breathing and the spiralling vortex of light. In this way, you will stay fully centred – truly 'at one' with yourself.

Soon you will come to associate your pattern of breathing with enhancing your own sense of inner vitality, while also helping to focus your sense of personal resolve.

One of the breathing patterns I have found most useful for this centreing process is the so-called 'four-four' cycle. Here, you breathe in to a silent count of four, hold to a count of four, release your breath to a count of four, then once again hold to a count of four. And so the cycle continues. This pattern of breathing has both a relaxing and an energising quality, and can also be accompanied by positive affirmations.

Positive affirmations for creating good karma

In modern everyday life, many of our negative thoughts and actions spring directly from how we think and feel about ourselves. For this reason, as we seek to create good karma, we should begin to focus on the positive rather than the negative aspects of our lives, while also taking time to reflect on the impact of our individual thoughts and actions on those around us. We can do this by making positive affirmations aimed at enhancing both the quality of our own life as well as our relationships with other people.

Affirmations can be defined as concise, accurate statements that describe our personal goals. The most effective affirmations are always those you create yourself that draw on your own knowledge and experience. An affirmation is essentially a positive statement you make to yourself in order to strengthen and reinforce your beliefs. It can relate to you, to other people, or to any issue of personal concern.

Affirmations only work if you are truly willing to integrate the goals expressed in the affirmation – both within your personality and also in everyday life. You can repeat your affirmations several times a day on a regular basis, write them down, or express them out loud. With time, the positive statement you are making in your affirmation will begin to de scribe how you really are and will not feel like an attitude superimposed from outside.

The essential characteristics of affirmations are as follows:
- They must be written in the first person
- They must be in the present tense
- They must relate directly to your personal goal
- They should be positive
- They should contain words that have good personal associations
- They should be specific, accurate and realistic
- They should be powerfully expressed and convincing

Affirmations should begin with the words 'I am' or 'I have, etc.' and should indicate that the goal has already been achieved. Here are some examples of positive affirmations oriented towards creating good karma:

- I accept who and what I am in the present moment
- I am calm and even-tempered
- I am an open channel of spiritual energy
- I offer my talents and abilities in the service of others

You may also find it helpful to combine silent affirmations with the deep breathing technique we referred to earlier. Breathe into your abdomen, hold your breath as you mentally repeat your affirmation, then breathe out, feeling as you do so that your positive affirmation has enriched all aspects of your physical and emotional well-being.

How Karma Influences Our Relationships

So far, we have emphasised that each one of us is responsible for creating our own karma, and that all our thoughts and actions will have a cumulative positive or negative effect sometime in the future. To this extent, we all help to create our own reality. However, this is placing the focus specifically on ourselves – or at least, on that image of the self we personally identify with on a day-to-day basis: our persona, or ego.

However, if we pause to reflect for a moment, we will see that none of us ever lives in total isolation, even though at times when we are angry or depressed, we may feel really cut off and withdrawn from other people. Although karma is generated through our individual thoughts and actions, we are all enmeshed in a broad web of relationships – with our loved ones, our friends, our work colleagues, and even with those whom we don't especially like or who are actually hostile or antagonistic towards us. (In this last instance, it is the exchange of negative thoughts and emotions that feeds and maintains our connection.) So, through our physical interactions with other people, and as a direct consequence of the thoughts and feelings that arise through our personal relationships, we continue to generate a flow of positive or negative karma. As we have already seen, this flow of energy develops a momentum of its own! Sooner or later, the good or bad karma we have created through our relationships will produce an outcome in our everyday lives.

We are all one 'family'

With regard to our karmic relationship with others, the Dalai Lama offers a fascinating insight on the need for tolerance and compassion in our dealings with other people. In his view, in the same way that we naturally feel an instinctive bond with members of our own immediate family, we should also extend this feeling of connection to the broad sweep of humanity, because through our numerous lifetimes on this earth – experienced through the endless cycles of rebirth – we are actually all related to one other! Our father or mother in this lifetime may have been our son or daughter in an earlier life. Our friend, neighbour or antagonist this time around may have been someone we knew in an earlier period. Similarly, the sense of trust, closeness, enmity or resentment we experience now may be the karmic consequence of something that happened a long time ago.

In the final analysis, says the Dalai Lama, we are all one family – one collective consciousness – whether we choose to recognise it or not. This means that in a karmic sense, we have to learn to work through our countless interactions with one another – whether in love or in war, in friendship or compassion, or alternatively, through emotional responses of hostility, resentment, jealousy or envy – until we finally realise that all our challenges and battles are really with ourselves. In a universal and spiritual sense, we are one another – we are all connected and interrelated as we undertake our ongoing spiritual journey upon the wheel of life and rebirth. We will continue fighting one another, loving one another, hating one another and embracing one another, in a continuing cycle that will continue for endless eons to come – until we finally achieve a state of karmic liberation. This state of liberation, sometimes referred to as mystical transcendence, will come about when we finally rise above the illusion that we are separate beings living separate lives in our own little separate worlds. According to the karmic wisdom tradition, our sense of 'separateness' is a deception that our everyday existence thrusts upon us, and that most of us embrace as true. Our destiny is finally to learn the lessons of our positive and negative karma, and to rise above the illusions that enmesh us in everyday life. According to karmic tradition, this is the only way we can experience reality.

Individual and collective karma

We can see now that because everyday life involves individual people as well as groups and webs of relationships, the law of karma can be recognised on both an individual and a collective level. Sometimes the lessons of history also seem to tell us that whole groups of people – tribes, societies, nations – create their own good and bad karma. As the well-known Zen teacher Philip Kapleau has expressed it: 'Joy or suffering can also follow from collective karma, in which each member of a group reaps according to what the group as a whole has sown.'

Our own period of history provides us with several negative examples of collective karmic consequences. In the Balkans, the cumulative tribal enmity of Serbs and Albanians, which in turn stretches back through many centuries, erupted into open warfare with catastrophic results. The tragic and ongoing conflict between Jews and Palestinians over tribal landmarks and territories has the same sense of karmic destiny about it – brought further into focus through the clash of different spiritual faiths. With similarly tragic consequences, in the mid-20th century Adolf Hitler was able to galvanise the German psyche and plunge his people into devastating international warfare.

These are certainly extreme examples but they remind us nevertheless that both individual and collective karma take their toll on everyday life. The spiritual lesson that emerges from the concept of collective kar.ma is that we are all involved in a web of personal relationships with other people and we all contribute actively to the 'mind-set' and belief-system of the group with which we identify. Whether we are focusing primarily on our personal and family relationships, or whether we extend our web of relationships to include larger groups like social, business and political organizations – or even tribes and nations – we continue to create positive and negative karma on both an individual and a collective basis. We can choose to spread peace, compassion and inclusiveness on the one hand, or hatred, violence and destruction on the other. We can fill our hearts and minds with positive and creative thoughts and intentions, or we can generate a wide variety of negative emotions that will eventually spill over into acts of antagonism and violence.

Karma and Personal Development

Put simply, the path of karmic self-development means shifting our personal orientation away from the world of material attachment and negative acts and emotions, and moving our focus instead towards the realm of spiritual awareness. From a karmic point of view, this is not a matter of 'escaping' from the everyday world so much as learning to embrace what is true in an ultimate sense. According to the ancient wisdom teachings, Unity Consciousness, Spirit, or God (we can use different names for the same idea) is really all that exists. From a karmic perspective, what we take to be our own separate lives and personalities are really just a much smaller fragment of a vastly greater whole, and we should view them in this light. Our individual lives and dramas are like stories within a much bigger drama, and all of these stories are ultimately played out on the universal stage of life itself. Everyday life is governed by the law of karma, and in the ultimate sense, there is only one, all-encompassing reality that provides truth and meaning in the everyday world. When we achieve this realisation, when we realise that there is only one overriding reality – or Unity Consciousness – that transcends our individual lives and our sense of separateness, then we will be liberated from the law of karma.

The pressures of everyday life

Most of us in modern Western society learn early on that our survival in everyday life depends primarily upon establishing our ego, or persona – the self we present to the world – and playing it for all it is worth in an increasingly competitive and often unfriendly world that respects strength above weakness. As we grow up, we also learn that modern society seems to reward those who assert their needs and project their personal image most effectively onto others – whether at home, at school or at work. Our daily focus, more often than not, becomes one of ever-expanding ego-fulfilment, with a strong emphasis on individual careers and material gain.

Many of us become increasingly competitive – and often more aggressive – as we seek to get further ahead of our fellow travellers, and if we are inclined by nature to be devious or ruthless, we may also develop strategies that ensure our advancement is at the expense of others. At the same time, we probably also develop an increasing pride in our accumulated material possessions, which then become a form of tangible proof that all our efforts have been worthwhile.

According to the law of karma, all of this effort and all of this struggle is based on an illusion. In following these pursuits, we are chasing dreams and aspirations that, in the final analysis, divide us from one another, make us more selfish and greedy, and place more emphasis on material gain than the spiritual aspects of life like love, compassion and personal sacrifice.

Turning towards the source

Some interpreters of the law of karma maintain that people who are wealthy in this lifetime have achieved material prosperity now because in an earlier lifetime they were generous and selfless, and this is their reward. This must remain a matter of speculation. However, the karmic tradition emphasises that the real purpose of our lives is not to accumulate material goods and possessions; rather, it is to learn to understand our true nature, thereby eliminating the cause of suffering – and, as most of us are aware, the accumulation of material goods doesn't necessarily make us happy! To eliminate suffering and delusion means, from a karmic perspective, turning our focus towards the source of all life – spirit or soul – and learning instead to be nourished by the lessons of inner awareness. This means that, in our own way, we come to regard our lives as an inner journey in which our 'rewards' are more spiritual than materi.al. Gradually, we must learn to explore our true inner nature, rather than rely on our external social personality, and we must learn to do this in a way that will provide us with a sense of meaning and purpose in relation to the broader scheme of things. This is an approach to personal self-development that is potentially so far-reaching that it will eventually link us with all other living creatures in our immediate environment, and finally with the Universe as a whole.

Changing our focus

When we add this depth of perception to our daily lives, our social and business activities take on an altogether different character. It is then not so much a matter of endlessly competing against others in order to feel personally fulfilled, but rather an ever-developing process of working in tandem with our fellow travellers. This involves acknowledging personal strengths and weaknesses in different individuals while recognising that all aspects of human endeavour are eventually part of a much broader spectrum of awareness and activity that finally transcends the efforts of any particular individual. From this broader viewpoint, we can finally recognise a shared sense of purpose for all human beings upon the planet.

Turning Karma into Dharma

The Eastern concept of dharma parallels and complements the idea of karma. Dharma encompasses the moral order, your personal duty as an individual, and a commitment to ethical and compassionate behaviour – it is all of these things combined. Translated into a Western context, the concept of dharma means attuning your actions to a truly spiritual perspective and doing the right thing in a particular context or situation. Buddhists often refer to dharma simply as 'the Way', while a Christian devotee might refer to dharma as 'following God's will'. However, dharma is more than just personal duty alone, for it involves purifying the mind and undertaking the quest for wisdom and spiritual insight.

The forces of past and future

According to the Eastern wisdom traditions, we should consider karma and dharma together, because they are like twin forces operating in our everyday lives. When a person is born according to the reincarnational perspective, that person brings to his or her new life all the karmic implications of what has taken place in earlier lifetimes. However, dharma relates to what the person needs to do now, both ethically and spiritually, in the present lifetime – because this will have consequences later on. As the Theosophical writer Annie Besant has expressed it, karma 'pushes us from the past' while dharma 'pulls us from the future'.

We are all shaped by our past, but we also have an obligation to create a better future – for ourselves and those around us, and also for the world as a whole. The law of karma demonstrates that in our everyday lives, none of us is ever truly separate or isolated. Karmically, through our thoughts and actions, we influence not only ourselves but others as well. This is where the idea of personal obligation or dharma assumes special importance, because each of us has social responsibilities that extend beyond what we do and think as individuals. In the Bhagavad Gita, Krishna tells Arjuna to 'strive constantly to serve the welfare of the world', and to act without selfish attachment, because to do this is to act in freedom.

Embracing life as a whole

According to the laws of karma and dharma, the whole purpose of the moral or ethical life is to promote what is basically good. This means that when we are deciding what we feel is right or wrong, the choices we make should not relate purely to our own concerns. We should also bear in mind the consequences of our thoughts and actions on other people. Truly moral or ethical choices are choices we make with others in mind, and are ultimately choices we make on behalf of all life as a whole. As the theologian and philosopher William Metzger has written, 'From a moral perspective, dharma is our duty to the One Life. It is not our duty to our self, our family, our employer, or our country isolated from others; it is our duty to all of life.... the One Life of which we are all part.'

Breaking free from our conditioning

None of us is destined to remain trapped in our karmic past. Dharma provides us with the option of breaking free from our past conditioning in order to achieve greater good – for ourselves, for those around us, and for the world as a whole. If karma sets the stage for who and what we are when we come into the world, dharma allows us to rise up to the next stage of spiritual development. Dharma allows us to outgrow the patterns of the past and break free from our past conditioning. Therefore, an important key to the spiritual life is learning how to turn karma into dharma.

Turning karma into dharma

Turning karma into dharma means following what Buddhists call 'the path of right action'. The right action for any particular individual involves responding to the world through all of our faculties, including all of those potentials of spiritual awareness that become available through practices like meditation and visualisation. At the same time, we begin to replace our 'lower human impulses' with what we might regard as a higher and nobler perspective. In this context, acting nobly means serving the world rather than just ourselves. It means that in our own way, we are helping to make the world a better place. Some of us may fulfill our dharma by playing an active role in a spiritual organisation or by assisting others with their spiritual practice or personal development. Fulfilling our dharma may also involve extending our commitment to the environment, serving in underprivileged communities, or interacting in a positive and compassionate way with those less fortunate than ourselves.

Dharma

The specifics of dharma are up to us, and the variations are endless, but the spiritual intent is all-important. The Dalai Lama has recently summed up some key elements in helping us cultivate what he calls 'a sense of universal responsibility':

- Become sensitive to others, not just those closest to you
- Stay honest in your thoughts and actions
- Avoid causing divisiveness among those around you
- Develop an attitude of mind where, if see you an opportunity to help others, you will choose this option rather than your own self-interest
- Cultivate a sense of contentment as being crucial to maintaining peaceful coexistence with others. This will enhance your sense of tolerance
- Respect other people's equal right to happiness
- Remember that we all have a duty of care towards our fellow human beings because we are all members of the human family

Karma, Fate and Destiny

Let's return for a moment to an issue that we skirted over at the beginning of this book – the issue of fate and destiny. Many people have equated karma with fate and destiny, and for some, the whole idea of karma means that we become slaves to what has happened in the past. For others, the concept of karma means that our past thoughts and actions dictate our future, and therefore our future is 'predestined'.

We have just discussed the idea of dharma, which clearly indicates that we always have the option to break free from the conditioning of the past and rewrite our future. Such options have everything to do with exercising our free will. Through our thoughts and actions, we assume the responsibility for helping to create a future that we share with others.

Clearly, if this is so, our future is not mapped out for us, or predestined. A predestined future is what many people refer to as their 'fate'. If someone experiences a run of misfortune, it is sometimes said that this was 'fated' to happen. Similarly, if they are involved in a serious accident, it is their 'fate' that determined that this accident would occur.

However, karma is not the same as 'fate' or 'predestination'. The concept of fate implies that we are bound by a power beyond ourselves that somehow restricts us and ensures that we will experience specific life circumstances that have been set out for us beforehand. Fate implies that we are so bound by these external circumstances that no personal effort of our own will make any difference whatsoever to the outcome. This, however, is not what the laws of karma and dharma are telling us. According to these spiritual laws, we have the power to shape and build our own future, and we will reap the consequences of our actions – good or bad – at a future time.

Fate and destiny

Although it is incorrect to equate fate and karma, it makes sense to link karma and destiny. Fate and destiny are not the same thing – fate is fixed, whereas destiny is changeable. As the twin forces of karma and dharma weave their way through what mystics often refer to as 'the dance of life', our personal destinies unfold before us as a consequence of what we have done in the past and what we are doing now. Even so, we are always able – through acts of individual free will – to create different outcomes through our personal thoughts and actions.

Selfish thoughts and actions will create a personal destiny based on the outcomes of these negative intentions, while virtuous actions will create positive outcomes and a positive destiny. In this way, the law of kar.ma helps us to learn from the lessons of life itself. As one writer has put it, 'In reality, all sets of circumstances are opportunities for us, for they are the natural results of past living and should be viewed as the steppingstones for our future growth. Our destiny is not imposed on us. It is of our own making, and we daily weave the threads of our future destiny.'

Weaving a collective destiny

We have already emphasised the fact that we are never truly isolated, for each and every one of us is part of a web of relationships. Some of these relationships are close and intimate – like the relationships we have with our friends, lovers or members of our immediate family. Other relationships are slightly more removed, like those we have with our neighbours or the people we work with in the office each day. Even further removed, but nevertheless still part of our immediate social fabric, are those fellow human beings who reside in the community, state, and country where we live. We can then reflect on the fact that all countries in turn make up a family of nations, and that these nations are increasingly interconnected through economic globalisation and international trading relationships, through global communication tools like television and the Internet, and through political organisations like the United Nations. So, does this mean that couples, families, communities and nations have karmic destinies as well as individuals?

According to the Eastern wisdom traditions, this is indeed the case. Couples and families are linked together through the bondings of their previous karmic relationships, which can involve consequences based both on mutual happiness or mutual suffering. From the karmic perspective, it may well be that couples who are married in this lifetime have come together in order to develop their spiritual potential togeth.er, and that this is part of their life-purpose. Alternatively, perhaps they were enemies last time around and are now seeking to work through the consequences of their shared destiny! In both instances, their relationship now may have come about as a result of thoughts and actions that occurred in a previous lifetime.

Family members may also connect with one another and reincarnate through numerous cycles of birth, death and rebirth. In the East, this concept is widely accepted as a fact of human existence. Families do not just happen by chance, but arise through an accumulation of shared destinies; here, too, the individual karmic links can be both positive and negative. Family members may have known one another, and been connected in various patterns of relationship, through many different circumstances and in many different times and places in history.

Nations also seem to create their own karma, producing a collective destiny that flows from the national psyche itself. As the Japanese psychologist and consciousness researcher Dr Hiroshi Motoyama has observed, 'Each nation on earth has its own Spirit, and that Spirit has its own karma … The karma of the National Spirit affects everyone living in the country, whether they are born there or immigrate from other places.'

We have already mentioned the war in the Balkans and the ongoing disputes between Jews and Palestinians as having a distinctly karmic dimension. It seems likely that such forces played a strong role in the nationalist fervour aroused by Adolf Hitler during World War Two. We may yet see further national karma play itself out in the political interactions between China and Tibet, in which both political and spiritual issues are at stake.

Finally, we must consider the karma of the planet as a whole. We live in a world of finite resources and vast social and economic inequalities. Our collective approach in recent times has been to draw on global resources as if they somehow extended into a timeless future, and yet clearly this is not the case. Issues like global pollution, the equitable distribution of food, respect for human rights and the need for religious tolerance are not just social and political concerns, but are also karmic concerns as well. In this sense, we are all contributing to collective karmic outcomes as well as weaving our own individual destinies. Sooner or later, we will all have to realise that we are all in this world together, and that future outcomes depend on individual and collective decisions taken now.

How to Develop Good Karma

According to spiritual teachers like the Dalai Lama, you can develop good karma by acting ethically and morally – by following the path of dharma, or 'right action'. One of the most important things to aim for in life is to develop the spiritual insight to understand the true nature of the human condition and the origin of suffering. Although this is something that may take us many years or even a number of lifetimes to achieve, this is the essential goal. Let us recall, once again, the central teachings of the Buddha:

- Cease to do evil
- Learn to do good
- Purify your own mind

We can take as a starting point the principle that we all have the right to experience happiness in our own lives; we can then extend this principle to recognise that everyone else has the right to experience happiness in their lives as well. This means that we all have an ethical and moral obligation to reduce the suffering of others. If we harm other people, we are acting unethically, and if we act unethically, we accumulate bad karma. On the other hand, acting to help other people without expecting reward – acting purely from the perspective of dharma – attracts good karma.

Seeking true happiness

Happiness in a spiritual sense means developing a sense of contentedness born of being essentially at one with the world and with all sentient beings. Happiness in this context doesn't mean sensory indulgence or the sort of transitory thrill of happiness and excitement you might experience by winning the lottery. In this last case, we would have to assume that the happiness came from the newfound wealth itself, and clearly that is not the case – because happiness is a state of awareness, not something physical. From a karmic perspective true happiness comes from within, arising as a consequence of our mental, emotional and spiritual balance. While we each experience such states of happiness in our own way, as a first step, we can begin by actively pursuing a state of contentment and inner peace and by making a personal commitment to avoid causing harm to others. We can also consciously undertake to ease suffering generally, both within ourselves and also in those with whom we are in relationship. This goes back to the idea that we should consider the impact of our thoughts and actions on other people and not act simply with selfish intent.

Character building

Working positively on our attitudes in this way is sometimes called 'character building'. There is a well-known saying that goes like this: 'Sow a thought and you reap an act; sow an act and you reap a habit; sow a habit and you reap a character; sow a character and you reap a destiny.' Work on becoming more aware of the consequences of your thoughts and actions on those around you, and begin to take a more long-term view of life in general. Begin to haul those bad habits back into line, taking a long, hard look at yourself. What are your admirable qualities? What things do you think and do that bring hurt and distress to those around you? How can you make things better, and so reduce the negativity that you bring to other people's lives as well as to your own?

Changing our values

If we follow Buddha's advice and make a true effort to 'cease to do evil' and 'learn to do good', we will in effect be changing our values – those particular beliefs and qualities that provide a context for our thoughts and actions. So, if you have decided to take that first step towards positive self-transformation, you may like to begin by making a list of all the things you like about yourself, with a focus first of all on your positive attributes. Are you generous and kind to others? Are you tolerant when faced with opinions and perspectives that differ from your own? Do you remain mindful of the consequences of your thoughts and actions on other people? Now make a list of the things you don't like about yourself. Perhaps you have a mean, resentful streak in your character, or a short fuse and explosive temper that can burst forth at any time. Maybe you are so ambitious that your social or material advancement is at the expense of others, or perhaps you value status and possessions more than people.

Now, finally, make a list of those things that you regard as negative aspects of your personality and behaviour but which you are willing to change. You might also like to take note of how these changes will benefit those around you. Then, finally, think of some things you can do now that will bring a positive change or benefit to someone you don't even know – perhaps someone in another community or country who is less well off than you.

If you work through this process, making a conscious decision to change for the better, you will certainly begin to attract good karma. You can also work on developing your capacity for tolerance, patience and compassion still further. If in this process you get into the positive habit of seeking peaceful mediation in any conflicts you may be experiencing, rather than adopting a confrontational perspective in your relationships at home or at work, you will be making your own small contribution to world peace! Much of this has to do with adopting a positive intent to change ourselves for the better, so that this impulse for positive change can then produce a 'flow-on' effect among our friends and family, and even begin to radiate out into society as a whole. This is how personal and collective karma brings changes to our own lives and society as a whole.

How to Protect Ourselves from Bad Karma

Buddha offered this advice for protecting ourselves from bad karma: cease to do evil, learn to do good, purify your own mind. We have considered the first two instructions; now, we can explore the idea of purifying the mind. However, the intent here is not to promote one approach to meditation or spiritual realisation over another. Rather, it is a call for each of us, in our own way, to seek our own spiritual centre – our core inner truth – because it is at the deepest level of our being that we experience the universal dimensions of the Spirit. Because we are all finally interconnected as fellow travellers on planet Earth, whether we acknowledge this or not, purifying our minds becomes a type of spiritual ecology. Purifying our minds is like clearing the psychic and spiritual atmosphere! It brings a positive ambiance to our everyday lives, which helps bring a positive and holistic dimension to our activities at home and in the workplace.

We can begin to purify our minds by undertaking some form of spiritual practice or by aligning ourselves with a proven spiritual tradition that leads to a deeper holistic awareness and experience of the sacred. Many different spiritual traditions and practices lead finally towards the universal spiritual experience that some call Oneness with God and others know as Self-Realisation or Unity Consciousness. These practices can be found within the spiritual traditions of both East and West, including Buddhism, Hinduism, Christianity, Islam and Judaism – although you may have to spend some time finding the particular path that is right for you. On page 90 is a simple self-purifying visualisation that will help you get started.

Opening Yourself to the Spirit

Sit down in a comfortable, meditative position, with your back straight and your hands resting in your lap. Close your eyes and breathe deeply, so you are now completely relaxed. Now visualise a ball of radiant white light immediately above your head. Imagine that this ball of light represents the pure spiritual light of the Universe – the light of true healing and transformation – and that this light is about to descend into your body and purify your inner being. Breathe deeply in and out, now visualizing this ball of light descending into your head, radiating purity, health and vitality in all directions.

Now watch with your mind's eye as you draw this ball of light down into your throat. Continue to breathe in and out, deeply and regularly, as you absorb the spiritual healing radiance into this part of your body.

Now visualise the ball of light descending still further until it comes down into your chest. Feel now that your body is truly lit from within, and a wonderful purifying radiance extends to all regions of your chest. As you breathe in, you feel the reawakening of vitality, and as you breathe out, you feel that you are expelling any impurities or toxins that have been restricting your health and well-being until this moment of release. Draw the ball of light down still further so that it radiates its healing light just above your navel. When you have filled this region with light, bring the sphere down just below your navel, then, in turn, draw it down into your pelvic region. Once again feel the nurturing, restorative power of the light as it fills your body with its healing radiance. Imagine that this healing sphere of light has now reached down to your feet, grounding itself and vibrating like a pulse through the very core of your being. You feel deeply relaxed, and profoundly purified. The healing light now dwells fully within you …

Finally, give thanks for this gift of light; when you are ready, open your eyes and return to the everyday reality of your familiar surroundings.

As you move onto a path of spiritual self-transformation and begin to explore the Eastern or Western wisdom traditions, you may find yourselves drawn more towards practices that offer the potential for spiritual experience. At the same time, you may also find yourself less attracted to specific religious doctrines as you embrace the universal spiritual truths that underlie all major religions. Eastern meditative and yoga practices are now well established in the West, but it is also possible to find experiential paths within the Western religions as well, if this is your preference. Meditation is not exclusively Eastern and is also valued in the Christian tradition; also, Christian prayer groups exist that focus on spiritual healing. You may also find it helpful to explore the mystical traditions within Islam and Judaism – known as Sufism and Kabbalah, respectively – for these also offer paths to greater spiritual awareness and self-knowledge.

Making responsible spiritual choices

Whatever spiritual path you choose in life, it is nevertheless true that karma is your own individual responsibility – and you will create good or bad karma as a consequence of your thoughts and actions.

However, you can protect yourself from creating and accumulating bad karma by making responsible spiritual choices in your everyday life. As the well-known spiritual teacher Deepak Chopra has observed, when we assume the responsibility of becoming a conscious choice-maker, we begin to generate actions that are evolutionary both for ourselves and also for those around us: 'As long as karma is evolutionary – for both the Self and everyone affected by the Self – then the fruit of karma will be happiness and success.'

The first step is to become really aware of the choices you make each and every day. As a general practice, learn to focus your conscious awareness on the specific act of choice-making. When you have practised this self-awareness for a while and are about to make a specific choice, focus your thoughts on the consequences of the particular choice you are making. Ask yourself whether this choice will bring happiness and understanding to both yourself and also to those who will bear some of the impact of this particular thought or action. Finally, you may wish to draw on your inner intuitive reserves and look for a heartfelt response to whether you are doing the right thing or not. If your decision then feels right to you – if you get that positive 'heart' reaction as an instinctual response – go ahead and proceed with it. If you don't receive some form of inner guidance that this is the right thing to do, you may wish to pull back from acting on the particular choice you have made. In both instances, you are acting in a karmically responsible way. At the same time, you are protecting yourself from bad karma, because in adopting this approach, you are acting from the spiritual depths of your being, assuming full moral and ethical responsibility for your individual thoughts and actions.

Karma and intentionality

Of course, sometimes we get it right and sometimes we don't. The point is that karmically our intentions are all-important. If we act with good intentions but somehow things don't turn out as planned, we will not incur bad karma in that particular instance. It is not the misdirected individual thoughts and actions in themselves that build negative karma, but the energy of the negative intentions that propels them. Developing our awareness of conscious choice-making and intentionality not only helps build our sense of self-awareness and personal responsibility, but also helps protect against creating bad karma. Ultimately, the karmic message is quite straightforward: we should endeavour at all times to act consciously from the depths of our inner being, and we should learn to become fully aware of the impact of our personal choices on both ourselves and others. If our choices are made with positive intent, the outcomes of these choices will be beneficial and will attract good karma. To this extent, we help shape our own destiny. We really have no one to fear but ourselves.

Creating Good Karma

As we have emphasised throughout this book, each of us is ultimately responsible for creating our own destiny, and the law of karma guarantees that in due course, the outcomes of our thoughts and acts will match our intentions. Still, it doesn't hurt to have a checklist of the sorts of things that will attract good karma. It is probably unrealistic to suppose that we will do all of the things listed below each and every day. However, cumulatively, the following checklist should help to keep you on the right karmic track! Respect other people's equal right to happiness.

Daily checklist

- Respect other people's equal right to happiness.

- Don't cause harm to other living things. Remember, they have the same right to their lives as you do to yours.

- Respect your body – it is a temple of your spirit. Do not misuse your senses or do anything to harm the sacred balance of body, mind and spirit. That is your birthright as a living, thinking human being.

- Refrain from negative thoughts and negative speech, for these pollute the emotional and spiritual atmosphere.

- Refrain from taking drugs or drinks that will cloud your mind.

- Try to become sensitive to the needs of everyone around you, not just those who are closest to you.

- Try to keep your thoughts and actions both positive and honest.

- Don't take things that don't belong to you.

- Don't play people off against one another. After all, they are creating their own karmic destinies just as you are creating your own!

- Develop a caring attitude of mind so that if you see an opportunity to help others, you will choose this option rather than your own self-interest.

- Maintain peaceful coexistence with others – this will enhance your sense of tolerance and compassion.

- Remember that we all have a duty of care towards our fellow humans, because ultimately, we are all members of the same human family.

- From time to time, practise extending acts of kindness to someone who has hurt you or harmed you in the past.

- Think of something about yourself you would like to change for the better, and commit to making that change come true.

- Practice what Shakespeare recommended: to thine own self be true!